To Jo,

read one before our runs!.

We can do it!

love you
from
Claire
x x x x

100 DAYS OF MAGNIFICENT RUNNING QUOTES

RUN FAST AND RUN INSPIRED

Mariana Correa

Copyright Page

100 DAYS OF MAGNIFICENT RUNNING QUOTES

ISBN 1979881464

All rights reserved. This book or any portion thereof may not be reproduced or used in any manner without the express written permission of the publisher except for the brief book quotations for reviews in the book.

Scanning, uploading, and distributing of this book via the Internet or via any other means without the express permission of the publisher and author is illegal and punishable by law.

Only purchase authorized editions of this book. Please consult with your physician before training and using this book.

Acknowledgement

To my son, thank you for being such a wonderful inspiration to me.

About the author

Mariana Correa is a certified sports nutritionist and former professional tennis player. Mariana reached a career high of 26 in the world in juniors with wins over Anna Ivanovich (former #1 WTA in the world) and many other top 100 WTA players.

She competed successfully all over the world in over 26 countries and hundreds of cities including in London for Wimbledon, Paris for the French Open and in Australia for the world championships. She also represented Ecuador in Fed Cup, where the team reached the finals in their group.

During her career she was awarded the fair play award many times, proving to be not only an excellent player, but also a role model for other athletes.

Being an athlete herself she understands what it takes to be the best in what you love.

Mariana is a certified sports nutritionist with years of experience in proper nutrition and hydration for high performance athletes.

She combines her love and knowledge in sports and nutrition in this book to provide you with all the information you need to succeed.

Description

100 DAYS OF MAGNIFICENT RUNNING QUOTES is the BEST inspirational and encouraging book for any runner, jogger or sprinter. It has the most stimulating advice from the world's top runners and some of the best sports minds in history to motivate and zoom past the finish line.

With an extraordinary collection of the most inspirational running quotes from around the world you will improve your marathon training, 5k racing , boost your self-esteem and confidence, claim your inner strength , overcome your fears and make your dreams come true.

"Employ your time in improving yourself by other men's writings, so that you shall gain easily what others have labored for. " Socrates.

Words are powerful and can help you accomplish everything you have been dreaming of.

Get inside the mind of the best athletes in the world and find out what it takes to succeed.

Table of Contents

Acknowledgements

About the author

Description

Chapter 1: RUNNING INSPIRATION

CHAPTER 1
RUNNING INSPIRATION

"Run when you can, walk if you have to, crawl if you must; just never give up."—Dean Karnazes

"Running is about finding your inner peace, and so is a life well lived." — Dean Karnazes

"I don't run to add days to my life, I run to add life to my days." — Ronald Rook

"The point is whether or not I improved over yesterday. In long-distance running the only opponent you have to beat is yourself, the way you used to be." — Haruki Murakami

"Every morning in Africa, a gazelle wakes up, it knows it must outrun the fastest lion or it will be killed. Every morning in Africa, a lion wakes up. It knows it must run faster than the slowest gazelle, or it will starve. It doesn't matter whether you're the lion or a gazelle – when the sun comes up, you'd better be running." — Christopher McDougall

"We got better at running because our heads were expanding, thereby providing more ballast." — Christopher McDougall

"I'll be happy if running and I can grow old together." — Haruki Murakami

"For me, running is both exercise and a metaphor. Running day after day, piling up the races, bit by bit I raise the bar, and by clearing each level I elevate myself." — Haruki Murakami

"I run because if I didn't, I'd be sluggish and glum and spend too much time on the couch. I run to breathe the fresh air. I run to explore. I run to escape the ordinary. I run…to savor the trip along the way. Life becomes a little more vibrant, a little more intense. I like that." — Dean Karnazes

"The Hopis consider running a form of prayer; they offer every step as a sacrifice to a loved one, and in return ask the Great Spirit to match their strength with some of his own." ― Christopher McDougall

"Some seek the comfort of their therapist's office, other head to the corner pub and dive into a pint, but I chose running as my therapy." — Dean Karnazes

"People sometimes sneer at those who run every day, claiming they'll go to any length to live longer. But don't think that's the reason most people run. Most runners run not because they want to live longer, but because they want to live life to the fullest. If you're going to while away the years, it's far better to live them with clear goals and fully alive then in a fog, and I believe running helps you to do that ." — Haruki Murakami

"If you don't have answers to your problems after a four-hour run, you ain't getting them." — Christopher McDougall

"Your body will argue that there is no justifiable reason to continue. Your only recourse is to call on your spirit, which fortunately functions independently of logic."
— Tim Noakes

"And one day, out of the blue, I started to run — simply because I wanted to. I've always done whatever I felt like doing in life. People may try to stop me, and convince me I'm wrong, but I won't change." – Haruki Murakami

"People think I'm crazy to put myself through such torture, though I would argue otherwise. Somewhere along the line, we seem to have confused comfort with happiness. Dostoyevsky had it right: 'Suffering is the sole origin of consciousness.' Never are my senses more engaged than when the pain sets in. There is a magic in misery. Just ask any runner." — Dean Karnazes

"All I do is keep on running in my own cozy, homemade void, my own nostalgic silence. And this is a pretty wonderful thing. No matter what anybody else says." — Haruki Murakami

"If you are losing faith in human nature, go out and watch a marathon." — Kathrine Switzer

"There is nothing so momentary as a sporting achievement, and nothing so lasting as the memory of it."
— Greg Dening

"First there came the action of running, and accompanying it there was this entity known as me. I run; therefore, I am." Unknown

"Running is real and relatively simple… but it ain't easy." — Mark Will-Weber

"How to run an ultramarathon? Puff out your chest, put one foot in front of the other, and don't stop till you cross the finish line." —

Dean Karnazes

"Ask nothing from your running, in other words, and you'll get more than you ever imagined." — Christopher McDougall

"It was being a runner that mattered, not how fast or how far I could run. The joy was in the act of running and in the journey, not in the destination." — John Bingham

"Getting more exercise isn't only good for your waistline. It's a natural anti-depressant, that leaves you in a great mood."
― Auliq Ice

"Try jogging when following your heart, it's healthier" — Benny Bellamacina

"What I've learned from running is that the time to push hard is when you're hurting like crazy and you want to give up. Success is often just around the corner." — James Dyson

"I'm often asked what I think about as I run. Usually, the people who ask this have never run long distances themselves. I always ponder the question. What exactly do I think about when I'm running? I don't have a clue." — Haruki Murakami

"But you can't muscle through a five-hour run that way; you have to relax into it like easing your body into a hot bath, until it no longer resists the shock and begins to enjoy it." — Christopher McDougall

"Adversity causes some men to break; others to break records." — William Arthur Ward

"Every run is a work of art, a drawing on each day's canvas. Some runs are shouts and some runs are whispers. Some runs are eulogies and others celebrations." — Dagny Scott Barrio

"I run because long after my footprints fade away, maybe I will have inspired a few to reject the easy path, hit the trails, put one foot in front of the other, and come to the same conclusion I did: I run because it always takes me where I want to go." —

Dean Karnazes

"The trouble with jogging is that, by the time you realize you're not in shape for it, it's too far to walk back."
— Franklin P. Jones

"If you don't think you were born to run you're not only denying history. You're denying who you are." — Christopher McDougall

"Jogging is very beneficial. It's good for your legs and your feet. It's also very good for the ground. It makes it feel needed."
— Charles M. Schulz

"Yes, I am round. Yes, I am slow. Yes, I run as though my legs are tied together at the knees. But I am running. And that is all that matters." —

John Bingham

"But I also realize that winning doesn't always mean getting first place; it means getting the best out of yourself." — Meb Keflezighi

"When I go to the Boston Marathon now, I have wet shoulders—women fall into my arms crying. They're weeping for joy because running has changed their lives. They feel they can do anything." — Kathrine Switzer

"The pain of running relieves the pain of living." — Jacqueline Simon Gunn

"When I was little and running on the race track at school, I always stopped and waited for all the other kids so we could run together even though I knew (and everybody else knew) that I could run much faster than all of them!" — C. JoyBell C.

"If you want to find the real competition, just look in the mirror. After a while you'll see your rivals scrambling for second place." — Criss Jami

"The finest of athletes have, along with skill, a few more essential qualities: to conduct their life with dignity, with integrity, with courage and modesty. All these, are totally compatible with pride, ambition, determination and competitiveness" — Donald Bradman

"Never underestimate the heart of a champion!" — Doc Rivers

"I could feel my anger dissipating as the miles went by–you can't run and stay mad!" — Kathrine Switzer

"There is about world-class athletes carving out exemptions from physical laws a transcendent beauty that makes manifest God in man." — David Foster Wallace

"Winning has nothing to do with racing. Most days don't have races anyway. Winning is about struggle and effort and optimism, and never, ever, ever giving up." — Amby Burfoot

"All truly great thoughts are conceived while walking." — Friedrich Nietzsche

"The thoughts that occur to me while I'm running are like clouds in the sky. Clouds of all different sizes. They come and they go, while the sky remains the same sky always. The clouds are mere guests in the sky that pass away and vanish, leaving behind the sky." — Haruki Murakami

"The reason we race isn't so much to beat each other, but to be with each other." — Christopher McDougall

"There is something magical about running; after a certain distance, it transcends the body. Then a bit further, it transcends the mind. A bit further yet, and what you have before you, laid bare, is the soul." — Kristin Armstrong

"Without running, I would have missed the joy of rain. What could be considered an inconvenience or a bummer to the inexperienced is actually a gift. Without running, I would miss a lot of things- like seeing cities in a certain way, or knowing certain people all the way to the core. I'm glad we don't experience life through glass, under cover, or from the sidelines. Good things take miles." — Kristin Armstrong

"Running is always an exercise in humility." — Kristin Armstrong

"Running has taken me in, and continues to comfort, heal and challenge me in all kinds of magical ways. I am not a 'good runner' because I am me. I am a good 'me' because I am a runner." — Kristin Armstrong

"A race is a work of art that people can look at and be affected in as many ways they're capable of understanding." -- Steve Prefontaine

"The best pace is a suicide pace, and today looks like a good day to die." – Steve Prefontaine

"Running is my private time, my therapy, my religion." – Gail W. Kislevitz

"The obsession with running is really an obsession with the potential for more and more life." – George Sheehan

"Pain is inevitable. Suffering is optional." – Haruki Murakami

"I often hear someone say I'm not a real runner. We are all runners, some just run faster than others. I never met a fake runner." – Bart Yasso

"Mental will is a muscle that needs exercise, just like the muscles of the body." – Lynn Jennings

"To give anything less than your best, is to sacrifice the gift." – Steve Prefontaine

"Somebody may beat me, but they are going to have to bleed to do it." – Steve Prefontaine

"Running! If there's any activity happier, more exhilarating, more nourishing to the imagination, I can't think of what it might be. In running the mind flees with the body, the mysterious efflorescence of language seems to pulse in the brain, in rhythm with our feet and the swinging of our arms." – Joyce Carol Oates

"Many people shy away from hills. They make it easy on themselves, but that limits their improvement. The more you repeat something, the stronger you get." – Joe Catalano

"Crossing the starting line may be an act of courage, but crossing the finish line is an act of faith. Faith is what keeps us going when nothing else will. Faith is the emotion that will give you victory over your past, the demons in your soul, and all of those voices that tell you what you can and cannot do and can and cannot be." — John Bingham

"Say you're running and you think, 'Man, this hurts, I can't take it anymore. The 'hurt' part is an unavoidable reality, but whether or not you can stand anymore is up to the runner himself." – Haruki Murakami

"Being active every day makes it easier to hear that inner voice. "
– Haruki Murakami

"If you always put limits on everything you do, physical or anything else, it will spread into your work and into your life. There are no limits. There are only plateaus, and you must not stay there, you must go beyond them."– Bruce Lee

"Mistakes are always forgivable, if one has the courage to admit them ." – Bruce Lee

"To hell with circumstances; I create opportunities." – Bruce Lee

"I'll never, ever be full. I'll always be hungry. Obviously, I'm not talking about food. Growing up I had nothing for such a long time. Someone told me a long time ago and I've never forgotten it, 'Once you've ever been hungry, really, really hungry, then you'll never, ever be full.' So I'll always be hungry in some way, driven and motivated to get what I want." – Dwayne Johnson

"With drive and a bit of talent, you can move mountains." – Dwayne Johnson

"Think back 5 years ago. Think of where you're at today. Think ahead 5 years and what you want to accomplish. Be Unstoppable." – Dwayne Johnson

"Having your health is having everything in life." – Brock Lesnar

"You, me, or nobody is going to hit as hard as life. But it ain't about how hard you hit. It's about how hard you can get hit and keep moving forward."– Sylvester Stallone

"Remember the mind is your best muscle. *Big arms* can move rocks, but *big words* can move mountains. Ride the brain train for success."– Sylvester Stallone

"Your spiritual sense will make you either a winner or a loser."– Sylvester Stallone

"Every time I've failed, people had me out for the count, but I always come back." –
Sylvester Stallone

"I am not the richest, smartest or most talented person in the world, but I succeed because I keep going and going and going."– Sylvester Stallone

"When you're scared, when you're hanging on, when life is hurting you, then you're going to see what you're really made of."– Sylvester Stallone

"I take rejection as someone blowing a bugle in my ear to wake me up and get going, rather than retreat." – Sylvester Stallone

"I believe there's an inner power that makes winners or losers. And the winners are the ones who really listen to the truth of their hearts." – Sylvester Stallone

"Success is usually the culmination of controlling failures."– Sylvester Stallone

"Every champion was once a contender that refused to give up."– Sylvester Stallone

"I believe any success in life is made by going into an area with a blind and furious optimism." – Sylvester Stallone

"I have great expectations for the future, because the past was highly overrated."– Sylvester Stallone

"I'm always looking for a new challenge. There are a lot of mountains to climb out there. When I run out of mountains, I'll build a new one." – Sylvester Stallone

"Don't count the days; make the days count."
– Muhammad Ali

"If my mind can conceive it, and my heart can believe it—then I can achieve it." – Muhammad Ali

"Impossible is just a big word thrown around by small men who find it easier to live in the world they've been given than to explore the power they have to change it. Impossible is not a fact. It's an opinion. Impossible is not a declaration. It's a dare. Impossible is potential. Impossible is temporary. Impossible is nothing." – Muhammad Ali

"I hated every minute of training, but I said, 'Don't quit. Suffer now and live the rest of your life as a champion." – Muhammad Ali

"If you don't give up, eventually you will break the cycle and you will overcome any obstacle." – Lyoto Machida

"I'm not the best. I just believe I can do things other people think are impossible." – Anderson Silva

"The uncomfortable zone is very important for us. To feel uncomfortable is important to strengthen your spirit. Like the samurai say, if you feel comfortable you must search for the discomfort, don't look only for the easy way."
– Lyoto Machida

"Infuse heart, soul, spirit and passion because talent is not enough." – Dominick Cruz

"If you want to fly with the eagles you can't hang out with the crows." – Brock Lesnar

"There's no talent here, this is hard work. This is an obsession. Talent does not exist, we are all equals as human beings. You could be anyone if you put in the time. You will reach the top, and that's that. I am not talented, I am obsessed." – Conor McGregor

"I always ask myself, "Did I get one percent better today?" – Benson Henderson

"If you're unwilling to leave someplace you've outgrown, you will never reach your full potential. To be the best, you have to constantly be challenging yourself, raising the bar, pushing the limits of what you can do. Don't stand still, leap forward." – Ronda Rousey

"My success isn't a result of arrogance. It's a result of belief." – Conor McGregor

Printed in Great Britain
by Amazon